MENTAL HEALTH SUPPORT

LIVING WITH PSYCHOTIC DISORDERS

by Maddie Spalding

San Diego, CA

© 2024 BrightPoint Press
an imprint of ReferencePoint Press, Inc.
Printed in the United States

For more information, contact:
BrightPoint Press
PO Box 27779
San Diego, CA 92198
www.BrightPointPress.com

ALL RIGHTS RESERVED.

No part of this work covered by the copyright hereon may be reproduced or used in any form or by any means—graphic, electronic, or mechanical, including photocopying, recording, taping, web distribution, or information storage retrieval systems—without the written permission of the publisher.

Content Consultant: Sarah K. Keedy, PhD, Associate Professor of Psychiatry and Behavioral Neuroscience, University of Chicago

---

LIBRARY OF CONGRESS CATALOGING-IN-PUBLICATION DATA

Names: Spalding, Maddie, 1990- author.
Title: Living with psychotic disorders / by Maddie Spalding.
Description: San Diego, CA: BrightPoint, [2024] | Series: Mental health support | Includes bibliographical references and index. | Audience: Ages 13 | Audience: Grades 7-9
Identifiers: LCCN 2023012475 (print) | LCCN 2023012476 (eBook) | ISBN 9781678206703 (hardcover) | ISBN 9781678206710 (eBook)
Subjects: LCSH: Psychoses in children--Juvenile literature. | Psychoses in adolescence--Juvenile literature. | Psychoses in children--Treatment--Juvenile literature. | Psychoses in adolescence--Treatment--Juvenile literature.
Classification: LCC RJ506.P69 S63 2024 (print) | LCC RJ506.P69 (eBook) | DDC 616.89/500835--dc23/eng/20230417
LC record available at https://lccn.loc.gov/2023012475
LC eBook record available at https://lccn.loc.gov/2023012476

CONTENTS

AT A GLANCE   4

INTRODUCTION   6
   MANAGING SYMPTOMS

CHAPTER ONE   12
   WHAT ARE PSYCHOTIC DISORDERS?

CHAPTER TWO   26
   MEDICATIONS FOR PSYCHOTIC DISORDERS

CHAPTER THREE   36
   THERAPIES FOR PSYCHOTIC DISORDERS

CHAPTER FOUR   48
   LIFESTYLE CHANGES

Glossary   58
Source Notes   59
For Further Research   60
Index   62
Image Credits   63
About the Author   64

AT A GLANCE

- Psychotic disorders disconnect people from reality. There are many types of psychotic disorders.

- Psychotic disorders disrupt people's everyday lives. They affect people's thoughts, emotions, and behaviors.

- Psychosis symptoms can include delusions and hallucinations. These are called positive symptoms of psychosis.

- Delusions are beliefs that do not change even when evidence shows they are not true. Hallucinations involve seeing, hearing, or feeling things that are not really there.

- People with psychotic disorders may have difficulty communicating and showing emotions. These are examples of negative symptoms of psychosis.

- Medication is used to treat psychosis. It helps people manage their symptoms.

- Therapy is also helpful in treating psychosis. Therapists help people learn skills to change their thoughts and behaviors.

- Self-care is helpful too. When people take care of themselves, they can better manage their symptoms.

INTRODUCTION

MANAGING SYMPTOMS

Laura was in line at a café. She was waiting to meet a friend. Laura looked around. She tried to distract herself. She felt as if someone's eyes were on her.

The woman behind Laura cleared her throat. Laura realized this woman had been looking at her. The woman smiled. She said,

"Sorry to bother you. I just wanted to say that I like your jacket."

Laura's brain set off a warning signal. A voice in Laura's head said, *She might be plotting something.* Laura ignored the

A psychotic disorder such as schizophrenia can make it hard for a person to get out and socialize.

voice. She told herself the woman was just being nice. After all, Laura was wearing a stylish outfit today. She had on bright colors instead of patterns. Patterns could cause Laura to see shifting images that were not really there. This was a **symptom** of Laura's schizophrenia. Laura had to be aware of and manage her symptoms. Medications and therapy helped her do this. She had a therapy session later that day.

Laura smiled back and thanked the woman. Then Laura ordered her coffee. She sat to wait for her friend. She pulled out a textbook to study for an exam. She used

Focusing helps people handle their disorganized thoughts.

a highlighter to flag important information.

This helped her focus on her work instead of the voice in her head.

Laura's friend entered the café. Laura concentrated on their conversation.

With the right treatment, people with psychotic disorders can maintain healthy relationships and do things they enjoy.

Every now and then, she felt as if others were watching them. Still, Laura was able to stay focused. Her schizophrenia symptoms were often in the background. But Laura was able to manage them.

PSYCHOTIC DISORDERS

There are many types of psychotic **disorders**. Schizophrenia is one of them. Psychotic disorders separate people from reality. People may see, hear, or feel things that are not really there. They may believe things that are unlikely to be true. These disorders are treatable. People with psychotic disorders can live full, healthy lives.

1 WHAT ARE PSYCHOTIC DISORDERS?

Psychotic disorders disrupt people's everyday lives. They affect people's thoughts, emotions, and behaviors. Psychotic disorders can cause many symptoms. People may have **hallucinations**. People with schizophrenia often hear voices. The voices may sound like their friends or loved ones. The voices may tell people things that are not true. Ashley Smith has schizophrenia. She explained, "Sometimes I heard one voice. Other times I heard multiple voices. I remember the voices being very . . . mean.

Having hallucinations can be very distressing for people.

They told me I was a dishonor to my family."[1]

People with psychotic disorders may have **delusions**. For example, a person may think other people are controlling him. He may believe others are trying to harm him. In other cases, people may think they have special powers. They may think they are on an important mission.

Katherine Ponte has struggled with delusions. She believed she could see the future. Ponte thought the world was ending. She needed to share this news with everyone. She thought she could save the

People may experience paranoid delusions. They might believe someone is watching or plotting against them.

world. Ponte believed that she "was being guided by a greater power. I saw signs everywhere."[2]

PSYCHOSIS SYMPTOMS

Psychotic disorders may come with negative and positive symptoms.

TYPES OF SYMPTOMS

Positive Symptoms	Negative Symptoms	Cognitive Symptoms
Delusions Hallucinations Repetitive movements	Difficulty showing emotions Becoming socially withdrawn Lack of interest in people and activities Low energy and motivation	Memory problems Difficulty focusing Jumbled or confused thoughts Going off-topic

Psychotic disorders can come with many symptoms. People may have positive and negative symptoms. They can also have cognitive symptoms.

These are terms used to describe people's experiences. Positive symptoms are unusual experiences. They are added to the normal events people have every day. Symptoms include delusions and hallucinations. They are often not pleasant. They can cause a person a lot of **distress**. Negative symptoms reduce or take away from what people do or feel. They can make it hard for people to communicate. One example is having a hard time showing emotions. People may also have **cognitive** symptoms. These can include memory problems or difficulty focusing.

Negative symptoms can be hard to deal with. They can make it difficult for people to do daily activities. They can cause people to withdraw from others. In a study released in 2020, researchers asked people with schizophrenia about their symptoms. One person described their struggle with low motivation. They said, "Brushing teeth felt like climbing the biggest mountain."[3]

CAUSES OF PSYCHOSIS

There is not one single cause of psychosis. Changes in brain chemistry play a role. Dopamine is a chemical in the brain. Too much of it in some brain areas causes positive symptoms. Too little of it in other areas of the brain also seems to play a role.

Certain drugs may cause psychosis. These include cannabis and cocaine. **Toxins** can have these effects as well. Carbon dioxide is an example. Certain medications can also cause psychosis symptoms. Medical conditions may cause psychosis too. These include migraines, brain diseases, and severe head injuries.

OTHER FACTORS

Certain factors can increase a person's risk of developing a psychotic disorder. Having a family member with a psychotic disorder increases a person's risk. High levels of anxiety or stress can play a role too. People who experience trauma are also at risk. Trauma is an emotional response to a distressing event such as an accident.

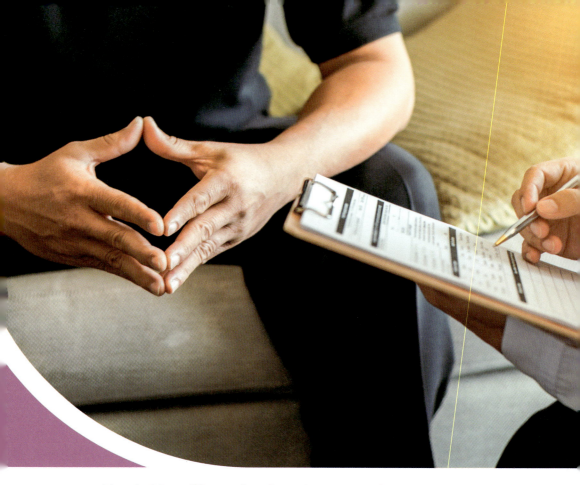

Mental health professionals ask patients about their symptoms before diagnosing them.

Sleep deprivation can cause psychosis as well. In some cases, the psychosis is temporary. But some people may develop psychotic disorders. This happens when psychosis affects their daily lives.

TYPES OF PSYCHOTIC DISORDERS

Mental health professionals **diagnose** people with disorders. People must have certain symptoms for a diagnosis. For instance, schizophrenia can have both negative and positive symptoms. A person must have symptoms for at least six months. People tend to develop symptoms in early adulthood. Common symptoms are hallucinations and delusions.

Some other psychotic disorders are similar to schizophrenia. But they do not last as long or affect people as much. Brief psychotic disorder lasts up to one month.

A stressful life event can cause this disorder. People with this disorder may have a hard time with short-term memory. They may behave out of character. These symptoms occur suddenly. Schizophreniform is another disorder. It lasts between one and six months. If either of these disorders lasts longer than six months, it is diagnosed as schizophrenia. Early diagnosis for psychotic disorders is important. It helps people find the right treatment.

    Schizoaffective disorder is another psychotic disorder. It is like schizophrenia. People have psychosis symptoms.

Supportive friends and family can encourage people to get help.

What makes it different from schizophrenia is that people also have depression or mania. People with depression feel hopeless. They feel sad. They have less energy. They also have trouble enjoying things. Mania is a period of increased energy. People are very active. They might not sleep as much. They may take more risks. Depression is more common than mania for people with schizoaffective disorder. People must have symptoms for two or more weeks.

Some people may have only delusions. These people can be diagnosed with delusional disorder if the delusions last at least one month. The person strongly believes these delusions. These beliefs guide the person's behavior.

People who are depressed may withdraw from loved ones.

Psychotic disorders affect people in many ways. But they can be treated. Treatment includes medication and therapy. People may also make lifestyle changes that can help.

2
MEDICATIONS FOR PSYCHOTIC DISORDERS

Medication is important in treating psychosis. Before the 1950s, doctors treated psychosis with tranquilizers. These drugs made people very sleepy and did not work well. Drugs made in the 1950s worked better. They decreased positive symptoms such as delusions. They did not cause as much sleepiness. But they had other side effects. They made people's movements slower.

Doctors later learned more about psychosis. They found out how dopamine plays a role. Scientists use this knowledge

Dopamine affects many things, including behavior, memory, attention, and cognition. It also plays a role in making people feel happy.

to develop medications. Medications that improve psychosis symptoms are called antipsychotics. They affect chemicals in the brain, such as dopamine and serotonin. Medications help the most with reducing positive symptoms of psychosis. They may also help with negative symptoms.

PSYCHOTIC EPISODES

Some people have only one episode of psychosis. This happens with brief psychotic disorder. Others have more than one episode. This happens with schizophrenia and schizoaffective disorder. An episode is a time when symptoms are not managed. People lose touch with reality. They can be a danger to themselves or others. Then they may be hospitalized.

ANTIPSYCHOTICS

There are many kinds of antipsychotics. Doctors help people find medications that work best for them. Clozapine is an antipsychotic. The US Food and Drug Administration approved it in 1989. It worked well. But it had some side effects. These included weight gain, tiredness, and dizziness.

Other antipsychotic medications were made to help people. But newer medications have side effects too. These can include weight gain and difficulty staying still. Doctors can change doses or

People need to take their medication exactly as prescribed. A doctor or pharmacist can help explain any instructions.

medications to help manage side effects.

People may need time to get used to

medications. Once this happens, the side

effects may be reduced. Or they may go away.

It can take people a while to find the best medication for them. Michelle Hammer has schizophrenia. She shares her experiences with the disorder. She helps people understand mental health issues. She says, "It took . . . almost ten years to get me on the right medication. I'm glad that I finally am."[4]

Many antipsychotics come in pill form. Others are taken as shots. The pill medications are taken by mouth daily. The shots are usually taken once every two to four weeks. A doctor or nurse gives the shots. A benefit of the shots is that people take them less often. That can be easier to remember than a daily pill.

TAKING MEDICATION

People with psychosis often struggle to take medication. This is especially true with schizophrenia. People may not believe they have a mental illness. They may think they do not need medications. They could think medical professionals are trying to harm them. This is an example of a delusion. People may also stop taking

It's important for people to take their medication if they want their symptoms to become manageable.

medications because of the side effects. As many as 50 percent of people with schizophrenia stop taking their medication.

Medications are not usually a cure. People often still have some psychosis symptoms. For example, they may still hear voices. Medication helps people manage their symptoms. It can help reduce how often people have unpleasant psychosis symptoms. That can help them focus on positive thoughts.

LONG-TERM TREATMENT

People often take antipsychotics for a long time. If they stop taking medication, their symptoms may return in full force.

Negative psychosis symptoms are hard to treat. Medications do not have much effect. People who take medication may still struggle with motivation or social skills.

Without medication, people will continue to experience psychosis symptoms.

Social skills training can help. This training can be part of therapy. A well-rounded treatment plan includes both medication and therapy.

3
THERAPIES FOR PSYCHOTIC DISORDERS

Therapy is an important part of treatment for mental illness. It can be used along with medications. Combined medication and therapy is the best treatment for psychosis. Therapy involves talking to a professional therapist. This is a person who is trained to understand and treat mental illnesses. Therapists help people understand their thoughts, emotions, and behaviors.

Cognitive behavioral therapy (CBT) is one type of therapy. It can help people with psychotic disorders. CBT involves recognizing unhelpful thoughts. These are

Therapy can help someone with a psychotic disorder figure out warning signs of an oncoming episode.

With help from a trained professional, people can learn to recognize negative thought patterns and change them.

thoughts that cause distress. They can worsen mental health symptoms. With CBT, people learn to question these thoughts. For people with psychosis, unhelpful thoughts can come from hallucinations. For example, someone may hear a mean voice in her head. She may think someone is out to get her. This can make her anxious. A therapist can help her recognize that the voice comes from her mental illness.

Kate Hardy is a psychologist. She treats people with psychotic disorders. She is trained in cognitive behavioral therapy for psychosis (CBTp). Hardy helps people replace unhelpful thoughts with helpful ones. Hardy says, "We're never trying to convince somebody that their experience is not real. This is especially important with hallucinations because they *are* real. There's no denying that the person *is* experiencing a voice."[5] Instead, Hardy helps people learn to interpret their thoughts differently. She explains that a helpful thought could be, "This is my mind playing tricks on me."[6]

CBTp can also help with paranoia. Paranoia is a type of unhelpful thought process. It involves an extreme mistrust of others. For example, someone may think people are staring at him angrily. He may believe people are thinking mean things about him. A therapist can help the person find other explanations. The other people may be stressed or distracted. Finding other reasons can put the patient at ease.

People who are paranoid may be convinced someone is following them. This might make them more anxious and upset.

He may start to feel safe again. Then he will be better able to function.

SOCIAL SKILLS TRAINING

People with psychotic disorders may struggle with social skills. They may have

People can practice and improve their social skills in places like work or school.

a hard time communicating. Social skills training can help with this. This training is part of therapy. People may role-play scenarios. They learn how to communicate in different environments, such as a workplace. They practice these skills outside of therapy.

Communication difficulties can cause stress. People may become frustrated when others do not understand them. They may get angry and respond in unhelpful ways. Social skills training helps them respond differently. This training helps with verbal and nonverbal communication.

For example, people pay attention to their tone of voice. They learn to change their tone to fit the situation. They learn about eye contact and facial expressions. This can help people function better in social situations. It can also lower people's stress.

COMMUNITY SUPPORT

Some people with mental illness may also struggle with basic living skills. In these cases, assertive community treatment (ACT) can be helpful. With ACT, people have a treatment team. Therapists help people take care of their mental health. They teach people skills such as time management. Nurses and psychiatrists help people manage their medications. People with psychotic disorders may struggle with employment. They may also need help finding housing. Social workers help people find these and other resources.

Early treatment of psychosis is important. People who get treatment early tend to have better outcomes. First Episode

OTHER DISORDERS

People with psychosis often also have other disorders. Many have substance use disorders (SUDs). SUDs happen when people misuse alcohol or drugs. People may also struggle with depression or anxiety. Therapy and medications try to target and address all of a person's disorders. If treatment does not address all of the disorders, it will be harder for the person to recover.

Psychosis (FEP) programs can help. These programs treat people in their first episode of psychosis. Experiencing psychosis for the first time can be scary. Loved ones may not know how to respond. FEP programs help people understand the illness. A team of professionals works together. The team includes therapists and medical providers. They help people work toward recovery. This can include finding educational opportunities or employment.

In FEP programs, doctors teach people about medications. Therapists teach people skills such as social skills or CBT skills.

To help someone who has a psychotic disorder, loved ones should listen to and not judge the person. They can encourage the person to get professional help.

They also educate family members on how to give support. Research shows that family support reduces **relapse** rates by 25 percent.

4
LIFESTYLE CHANGES

People with psychotic disorders can make lifestyle changes. These changes may help them manage their symptoms. People can pay attention to their self-care. Self-care includes tasks people do to take care of themselves. Getting enough sleep and exercise are part of self-care.

So is taking medications. Managing stress and building self-esteem are part of self-care too.

Self-care can improve a person's physical and mental health. People who do not take care of themselves are at a higher risk for relapse. Having a daily routine is important.

Exercise can help people's mental and physical health. A simple jog around a park can improve a person's mood.

Showering is one example of a daily self-care routine.

This can reduce stress. It can help people remember to take their medications. Michael Hedrick has schizophrenia. He tries to stick to a daily routine. Exercise and relaxation are part of this. So is taking care of hygiene. He says, "A routine can help you make better decisions . . . and it can make life manageable. In my opinion . . . making life manageable is just as important as taking your meds."[7]

RECOGNIZING TRIGGERS

Another part of self-care is learning to recognize triggers. Triggers are anything that could lead to a psychotic episode. Lack of sleep and stress are common triggers. Alcohol and drugs can be triggers too. Journaling can help people learn about their triggers. It can also help people track their self-care.

People usually have warning signs of an episode. For psychosis, these signs include irritability, anxiety, and difficulty sleeping. Psychosis signs and symptoms can worsen suddenly for no reason. But they can also get worse if people don't meet their self-care needs. People can

OTHER WARNING SIGNS

Lauren Kennedy has schizoaffective disorder. She knows her psychosis warning signs. One sign is having a hard time with responsibilities. This can include not paying bills or missing appointments. She says, "When you're heading in the direction of psychosis, it can be really . . . hard to keep up with life."

Living Well with Schizophrenia, "10 Signs I'm Slipping into Psychosis," YouTube, September 26, 2020. www.youtube.com.

Being open with loved ones can help them understand what a person is going through.

examine their self-care practices when they notice warning signs. They can develop self-care strategies. For example, they could create a sleep schedule. They could try relaxation exercises such as deep breathing. Other self-care ideas include going on a walk or taking a shower. Sticking to a routine for taking medication is part of self-care too.

People with psychotic disorders may get to a point of crisis. They might have thoughts of harming themselves or others. People may not be able to take care of themselves or make good decisions. They can prepare for a crisis by creating a crisis plan. These plans can include people to call for support. Some people with psychotic disorders make a self-care box. They fill the box with comforting items such as photos.

Crisis plans help during emergency mental health situations. They can include crisis hotline numbers and addresses for nearby care centers.

FINDING MEANING

Low self-esteem can lead to relapse.

Finding meaningful activities can help. One example is volunteer work. This work can connect people to their communities. It can help them feel good about themselves. It can give people hope.

Support groups can also be helpful. These groups bring together people who have similar experiences. They can help people connect with others. Support groups can help people realize they are not alone.

Some people with mental illness choose to share their stories. They try to send a message of hope. Ashley Smith shared her experiences with schizophrenia. She leads mental health support groups. She also made a blog where she shares her story.

Support groups can be either virtual or in person.

She says, "I . . . share my story with other people so that they know they can recover as well."[8]

GLOSSARY

cognitive

having to do with thoughts or thinking

delusions

beliefs that don't change despite evidence showing that they are not true

diagnose

to identify an illness or condition based on its symptoms

disorders

physical or mental conditions that cause distress and affect a person's ability to function

distress

great strain or difficulty

hallucinations

psychosis symptoms that involve seeing, hearing, or feeling things that are not really there

relapse

to experience a full return of symptoms

symptom

a sign of a disease, illness, or disorder

toxins

poisonous substances

SOURCE NOTES

CHAPTER ONE: WHAT ARE PSYCHOTIC DISORDERS?

1. Quoted in LEAP Institute, "Living with Schizophrenia," *YouTube*, February 18, 2013. www.youtube.com.

2. Katherine Ponte, "My Reality During a Psychotic Episode," *NAMI*, June 12, 2019. www.nami.org.

3. Quoted in "Understanding Individuals' Subjective Experiences of Negative Symptoms of Schizophrenia: A Qualitative Study," *NIH*, April 3, 2020. https://pubmed.ncbi.nlm.nih.gov.

CHAPTER TWO: MEDICATIONS FOR PSYCHOTIC DISORDERS

4. Quoted in WebMD, "Voices, Living with Schizophrenia," *YouTube*, October 12, 2017. www.youtube.com.

CHAPTER THREE: THERAPIES FOR PSYCHOTIC DISORDERS

5. Quoted in Caroline Miller, "How Does CBT Help People with Psychosis?" *Child Mind Institute*, January 23, 2023. https://childmind.org/

6. Quoted in Miller, "How Does CBT Help People with Psychosis?"

CHAPTER FOUR: LIFESTYLE CHANGES

7. Michael Hedrick, "Living with Schizophrenia: The Importance of Routine," *Your Care Everywhere*, September 7, 2017. www.yourcareeverywhere.com.

8. Quoted in "Living with Schizophrenia." *YouTube*.

FOR FURTHER RESEARCH

BOOKS

Corona Brezina, *Jump-Starting a Career in Mental Health and Therapy*. New York: Rosen Publishing, 2019.

Jennifer Phillips, *What Are Psychotic Disorders?* San Diego, CA: BrightPoint Press, 2023.

Susan Wroble, *Living with Depression*. San Diego, CA: BrightPoint Press, 2024.

INTERNET SOURCES

"Overview—Psychosis," *National Health Service*, December 10, 2019. www.nhs.uk.

"Psychosis," *Mind*, January 2020. www.mind.org.uk.

"Psychosis," *National Alliance on Mental Illness*, 2022. www.nami.org.

WEBSITES

Early Psychosis Intervention (EPI)
www.earlypsychosis.ca

EPI shares information and resources for people experiencing their first psychotic episode. It also educates people about the benefits of early treatment for psychosis.

Mental Health America (MHA)
www.mhanational.org

MHA raises awareness of mental illnesses such as psychotic disorders. It also supports research and laws to help people with mental health issues.

National Alliance on Mental Illness (NAMI)
www.nami.org

NAMI educates people about mental health issues. It offers resources and information. NAMI also has a helpline. People can call NAMI for support.

INDEX

antipsychotics, 28–31, 34
anxiety, 19, 39, 45, 52
assertive community treatment (ACT), 44–45

brief psychotic disorder, 21–22, 28

CBTp, 39–40
cognitive behavioral therapy (CBT), 37–39, 46
cognitive symptoms, 16–17
crisis plan, 54

delusional disorder, 24
delusions, 14, 16–17, 21, 24, 26, 32
depression, 23–24, 45
diagnose, 21–22, 24
dopamine, 18, 27–28

exercise, 48, 50

First Episode Psychosis (FEP) programs, 46

hallucinations, 12, 16–17, 21, 38–39
Hardy, Kate, 39–40

journaling, 51

mania, 23–24

paranoia, 40

relapse, 47, 49, 55

schizoaffective disorder, 22–24, 28, 52
schizophrenia, 8, 10–13, 18, 21–23, 28, 31–33, 50, 56
schizophreniform, 22
self-care, 48–54
side effects, 27, 29–31, 33
social skills training, 35, 42–43
substance use disorders (SUDs), 45
support groups, 56

therapist, 36–37, 39–40, 44, 46
toxins, 19
trauma, 19
treatment team, 44
triggers, 51

volunteer work, 55

warning signs, 52–53